BUILDING SUCCESS IN READING AND

Struggling Readers

at Key Stage 2

Diana Bentley and Dee Reid

ISBN 0 435 57351 9

Cataloguing-in-publication data
A catalogue record for this book is available for the British Library.

GHPD

Published by GHPD
Ginn Heinemann Professional Development
Halley Court, Jordan Hill, Oxford OX2 8EJ
www.ghpd.co.uk

2001   2000   99

5   4   3   2   1

Design and artwork production: Serif Tree · Oxford
Illustrated by Vali Herzer
Printed and bound in Great Britain by Ashford Colour Press, Gosport, Hants.

Contents

Adam's Story

Adam lives with his mum on a large estate on the outskirts of a city. He was born in July and when he was nearly four he started at the local Nursery school. He enjoyed his time at Nursery. He liked playing with the outdoor toys and running around with the other boys. The Nursery teacher felt that at times he was a little too boisterous but that he was an outgoing child with a cheeky smile. His spoken language was immature and he tended to get cross when he could not make himself understood. He rarely participated voluntarily in sedentary activities such as painting, gluing and sticking or browsing in the book corner and he was restless and easily distracted during story time. He had one particular buddy but he showed little interest in making friends with a wider group of children.

At Easter he started at the local Primary school. The Reception class had 25 children in it and Adam appeared bewildered by the change of environment and the number of children. He found it difficult to settle to the more structured organisation of the school day. The results of the baseline assessment revealed that he could recognise his own name but his role play writing showed no evidence of knowledge of letters of the alphabet. He knew the difference between print and pictures but he showed no grasp of left to right orientation of letters and words.

In the Autumn term of Year 1 Adam's school attendance was patchy. He had a spate of colds and coughs. In Shared Reading he enjoyed joining in chanting repetitive refrains and liked answering simple questions. However, he didn't seem to cotton on to word level work and his phonological awareness of rhymes and letter sounds were poor. He tended to echo the answers provided by other children.

The Year 1 teacher's report on Adam at the end of the year noted that he read in context about 15 high frequency words but could only spell about 5 of these. He muddled some initial letter sounds and when forming letters many were inversed or reversed. His teacher commented that Adam was trying his best and that he was, on the whole, a happy and pleasant little boy although she had noticed an increase in boisterous behaviour in the playground.

At the start of Year 2 the school made a determined effort to improve Adam's literacy skills. His situation was brought to the attention of the Special Needs Co-ordinator (SENCO) who put Adam onto Stage 1 of the Special Needs Register. This identified areas of concern but his new class teacher felt that as he was young for his year he might make a breakthrough and she was reluctant to proceed with more formal aspects of remediation.

After Christmas his mother came to see the class teacher. She was obviously worried about Adam's lack of reading progress. She commented that he appeared to know words one day and not the next, and she suspected that he was not getting the help he needed. She also enquired whether the school thought he was dyslexic. After this visit the teacher noted that Adam was reluctant to take his reading book home and his enthusiasm for reading was waning. However, Adam did make some progress during the Spring term and his teacher felt that he might achieve a borderline level 2 assessment in the Standard Assessment Tasks (SATs) in the summer.

Accordingly she administered the oral reading assessment of the Key Stage 1 SATs and also entered Adam for the Level 2 Comprehension test. However, his performance on this test revealed that his slow reading and inadequate comprehension meant that he was awarded a Level 1, placing him in the bottom 25% of children.

When Adam moved up to the Junior School his Year 3 teacher, in consultation with the SENCO, placed him on Stage 2 of the Special Needs Register and drew up an Individual Education Plan (IEP) in order to give Adam the support he needed.

Adam has not settled well in Year 3. The Key Stage 2 curriculum with its expectation that children can read and write with some fluency has meant that Adam has become increasingly aware of the gap in achievement between himself and his peers.

The class teacher reports that his behaviour is deteriorating. He uses avoidance tactics during lessons and he is frequently in trouble with the dinner ladies for rowdy behaviour in the playground. Adam's class teacher is uncertain how to help him. Adam works in a group of weak readers and writers but when asked to work independently he wastes time and frequently distracts others. Adam's mum has also stopped trying to help him and has started to say he is uncooperative at home. Adam himself feels frustrated and angry. He says he hates reading and writing and that school is 'boring'.

The hopes of Adam's Early Years teachers that he would, in time, become a reader seem a distant dream. There seems little chance that he will ever achieve Level 4 in the assessments at the end of Key Stage 2.

In 1999 approximately 13% of children entered Key Stage 2 at Level 1. If these children are not provided with a manageable, focused intervention programme their educational future looks bleak.

It is for children like Adam and other similar children that this book has been written.

Why do Children Find Reading Difficult?

It is almost impossible to decide where things went wrong for Adam or why others like him find reading and writing so difficult. It is likely to be a compounding of problems each of which seemed insignificant at the time but all of which contributed to his overall failure.

Research into possible causes of reading difficulty is probably the most highly researched subject within education. The reasons for failure appear to be as diverse as the children themselves.

It is generally agreed that reading involves all of the following:

- recognise all letter shapes and names
- map letter sounds on to print
- learn how to segment words into sounds
- learn how to blend the sounds of the letters to form words
- to recognise a word and its lexical meaning
- to interpret the meaning of the word in its context
- to seek to understand the meaning of the text

If a child is unable to do any of these processes then he or she is likely to struggle with reading. Different remediation techniques have concentrated on one or more of these skills but it is only when all the processes are activated that successful reading ensues.

SPECIFIC LEARNING DIFFICULTIES (DYSLEXIA)

Some children appear to have problems with reading and spelling that are grouped together under the heading "Dyslexia" or "Specific Learning Difficulties". The nature of the problems that these children exhibit, (for example: an inability to master rhyme recognition; very poor sequencing skills; inability to repeat a nonsense word; an inability to recall a sequence of numbers and problems with automatic tasks such as balancing) means that they may require specialised help. The classroom teacher is advised to discuss children with these specific difficulties with the Special Needs Co-ordinator (SENCO). For further information contact The British Dyslexia Association (0118 966 8271).

HELPING THE DYSLEXIC CHILD IN THE CLASSROOM

Remember that children are rarely lazy. They may try to avoid a task if it seems far too difficult or they may play around if the task is too easy. Dyslexic children with good verbal intelligence are adept at hiding their difficulties and can appear lazy or uninterested. In the majority of cases they are trying very hard to produce the required work.

They can be helped by:

- ensuring that they have a small piece of card with their name clearly written on it

- by providing them with access to basic spellings

- by ensuring that the day and date are clearly written on a board for them to copy

- by using different colours to emphasise the relative importance of words / tasks e.g. underlining in red important sentences, marking in green important words

- by using different colours to label linked apparatus, e.g. Maths equipment

- by numbering the lines on a board or on worksheets. If they get distracted they can then quickly find where they are.

- by asking the child to repeat or explain the instruction you have given back to you

- by praising every success

I can assure you that I am adressing all aspects of the report genre

"Dyslexic children with good verbal intelligence are adept at hiding their difficulties."

Assessment

BASIC LITERACY SKILLS ASSESSMENT

Many children who find reading difficult do not have specific learning difficulties. Their problems are of a more general nature.

Before embarking on a remediation programme it is important to establish which basic literacy skills the child has acquired. Marie Clay in her Reading Recovery Programme recommends that thirty minutes a day for two weeks is spent discovering what the child already knows. The intention is that this gathering of information about a child required the teacher to stop teaching from preconceived ideas. Marie Clay (Observation Survey 1991 Heinemann) has shown that observation of a child is essential and the information gleaned from this observation must form the basis of all assessment. The teacher has to work from the child's responses, discovering what the child does well and what strategies the child uses. Identification of reading / spelling difficulties is only worthwhile if a programme of remediation is planned around the information.

(The photocopiable assessments on pages 32 to 43 may guide the teacher in the collection of this information.)

"Observation of the child is essential."

STANDARDISED TESTS

Many schools use Standardised Tests to assess their pupils' performance and to assign a Reading Age to each pupil. The statistical evidence of these tests is not in doubt but few of these tests are diagnostic in that they do not suggest *why* a child has got it wrong or *how* to help them to put it right, they merely position the child's reading ability in relation to other children of the same age. Too often the test information confirms what a teacher already knows, or if it is discrepant, many teachers explain the unexpected results in terms of the child having an 'off' day. If schools administer a standardised test they should ensure that the information it reveals is used as the basis to devise practical classroom activities which will help pupils overcome the identified problems.

Many weak readers appear to have made little or no progress between tests because the small amount of improvements they have made are absorbed by the passage of time. Teachers, pupils and parents can become demoralised at the apparent lack of progress. In reality these children have acquired new skills and these should be the basis for further classroom teaching.

The testing procedure at the end of Key Stage 1 has the potential to be a diagnostic assessment of oral reading, reading comprehension, evidence of unaided writing and provide evidence of spelling and handwriting scores. The Year 3 teacher should use this as a basis for planning support for weak readers. This range of reading and writing assessment is more valuable than the simple summary statement of performing at National Curriculum Level 1 or 2C.

ASSESSING ORAL READING

Traditionally at Key Stage 1 children's reading performance was assessed in the classroom by the teacher hearing an individual child reading a book judged to be at an appropriate level. This was undertaken as often as possible but with the pressure of class sizes this often meant hearing each child twice a week for 3–5 minutes per session. Frequently this teaching time consisted entirely of hearing the child read aloud and did not include any focused intervention based on miscues. This pattern is often continued for weak readers at Key Stage 2. Unfortunately this approach to teaching reading is insufficient. Children do need to read to the teacher as often as possible but to maximise the effectiveness of this session the teacher should analyse the child's strengths and weaknesses and teach the child based on this information. Hearing a child read for a few snatched minutes will not teach the child the necessary strategies.

It is significant that there is no endorsement of hearing children read on an individual basis within the Literacy Hour. This is because it is deemed to be an ineffective use of teacher time. However, many Key Stage 1 teachers and teachers working with struggling readers at Key Stage 2 continue to hear readers individually. This one-to-one teaching can be extremely effective if the time is used not only to diagnose miscues but also to teach to remediate the errors. For this to take place time slots of time in excess of 3 to 5 minutes are essential. A once a week 10-minute individual session may prove more valuable than more shorter sessions. Some teachers may be able to pair children of similar ability.

THE 10 MINUTE INDIVIDUAL TEACHING SESSION

> **Timing of the session**
>
> Prepared Reading: 2 minutes
>
> Hearing the child read: 4 minutes
>
> Teaching linked to identified miscues: 4 minutes

The Advantages of an Extended Individual Session

The benefit of providing a longer individual tuition time is that the child has the opportunity to employ strategies to decode the text and also has time to reflect upon the meaning of the text. Finally there is time to consolidate the recognition of words by learning to spell specific new sight words.

1. Prepared Reading

Prepared Reading is a method of sharing the content of a text before the child is required to tackle the decoding. The teacher selects a text at instructional level (90–95% accuracy) and swiftly turns the pages, telling the story of the pictures prompted by the written text. In this way the teacher subtly introduces the child to any problem vocabulary before the child attempts to read. This also ensures that the child has a grasp of the content before he or she begins reading. Many weak readers have very little concept of story. They do not necessarily expect events on one page to have any bearing on the subsequent pages. Their concern is to read the words on any particular page and because they are so concerned with correct decoding of words they do not simultaneously engage with the events of the story.

Weak readers are often very anxious about getting the words wrong. Competent readers make mistakes but because their goal is to make meaning of the text they confidently self-correct. Struggling readers often grind to a halt when faced with an unknown word. They are not attending to the meaning of the words they are reading so they have little chance of predicting an unfamiliar word.

Through Prepared Reading children are able to embark upon reading a text with prior knowledge of the characters and events. It provides an introduction to the language of the story and a grasp of the plot. This increases the pace of their reading and this in turn enables them to comprehend the meaning of each word in its context. This rapid exploration of the text should take about 2 to 3 minutes. Discussion during this time is not encouraged unless the teacher is concerned that the child does not understand any specific vocabulary. The following is an example of a Prepared Reading commentary.

Pete was a pirate.
He had a parrot called Beaky.
Pete had a map.
On the map was a treasure island.

2

One day Pete went to the island.
'I will find the treasure,' he said.

3

A prepared reading commentary for this page could go as follows:

"Look, here is Pirate Pete with his parrot called Beaky. Pete has a map. On the map I can see a treasure island. Pete is going to the island. He wants to find the treasure."

2. Hearing the child read – diagnostic assessment

Many weak readers lack confidence in any cueing strategies. When they read a text they read the words they already know and rely on the person hearing them read to tell them the unknown words. They have no expectation to be able to decode unfamiliar words, they seem to believe that there are words which you recognise and words which you do not, and when faced with an unfamiliar word they are helpless.

When we hear children read it is very important that they understand that it is their responsibility to tackle the words and that there are strategies they can employ to sort out an unknown word. Many of these children do have letter/phoneme knowledge but they seem unaware of the value of this knowledge when tackling unfamiliar words. We need to help these children to understand that sorting out an unfamiliar word takes time, and that a pause in the reading is not necessarily a bad thing if the time is being used to study the problem word. They also need to be flexible about mapping sounds to letters. An important concept to get across to these children is that attempting words is what good readers do and good readers reflect upon the attempt to see if it makes sense.

We need to give these children time to develop that confidence and to use their cueing strategies. They will not see the value of these strategies if the teacher supplies the problem word after a moment's hesitation.

As the child reads aloud the teacher should note any miscues and decide upon a teaching focus. Allow the child to read to you for approximately four minutes.

3. Teaching linked to identified miscues

Extended individual sessions need to include focused teaching arising from a specific miscue. This helps the child to see the relevance of the word and letter sound study in the context of a familiar text. Too often these children practise isolated word skills and do not link them to the words they attempted to read in a story.

The teacher should select a miscued word that she feels is valuable for the child to learn. She then asks the child to study the word and discuss ways of remembering it, before asking the child to write it from memory. This should be practised until the child can confidently read and spell it.

"This should be practised until the child can confidently spell it."

Struggling Readers in the Literacy Hour

Although it is very important that Struggling Readers receive focused individual tuition, these children also need to be supported during all phases of the Literacy Hour.

The Literacy Hour provides the opportunity for a variety of reading and writing experiences. Each part of the hour has its own teaching and learning focus. In Shared Reading and Writing the teacher's role is to model how to read, write and interpret text. The children are **dependent** upon the teacher making the text accessible.

In Guided sessions the teacher's role is to support the children's reading and writing. The children work **interdependently**.

In Independent work, the children work **independently** consolidating their learning.

Each week should be a balance beween these teaching and learning styles.

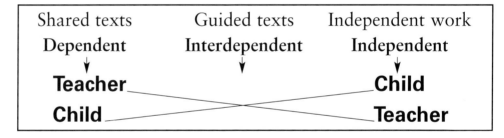

This model of teaching and learning is very beneficial to weak readers, providing, as it does, frequent models of good reading stategies, combined with focused support within the group before the children tackle a text independently.

SHARED READING – TEXT LEVEL

The National Literacy Strategy advises that the texts used for Shared Reading should be rich and challenging and beyond the ability of some of the class. For struggling readers this can mean that they are puzzled by the content and language of the text and even after multiple re-readings they may only have a surface understanding. They may be able to respond generally to the plot and theme but they are unlikely to have a more sophisticated level of comprehension.

It is important that these children are encouraged to participate to the best of their ability.

- Ensure that they sit at the front of the group so that you are aware of how much attention they are paying in the lesson.

- Often these children are not certain which words or phrases are the most significant. Point out the important parts of the text, perhaps by underlining those words you want the children to notice particularly.

- Ensure the children have followed the plot and characters by asking them simple literal questions.

- Allow weak readers the opportunity to hear how more confident readers respond. It may be possible to ask able readers on Monday some searching questions and to ask less able readers the same questions a few days later.

- Give weak readers enough time to respond to a question. One technique to build their confidence is to allow children to discuss their answers with a partner before answering in front of the whole class. Hopefully this encourages children to listen to one another's answers as well as to the teacher's questions.

- Struggling readers benefit from many revisits to the Shared Text (even beyond the class shared time) and making a recording of the text for them to listen to in independent work will increase their familiarity with the challenging text and should give them further confidence in subsequent shared sessions.

SHARED WRITING – TEXT LEVEL

Shared Writing provides the opportunity for the teacher to model a particular genre of writing. For some able children this modelling can be sufficient stimulus for them to attempt a related task on their own. Weak writers will need much more support and the content of many guided writing sessions will be working carefully through the stages of structured support.

The National Literacy Strategy has identified stages of teaching and learning when introducing a genre.

1. Familiarisation

Initially pupils are shown many examples of the genre. This can take place in Shared work and also in Guided sessions.

2. Problem solving

The teacher guides the pupils into identifying the salient features of the genre. For example, the children may state that: "All recipes have a list of the ingredients". These statements are checked for accuracy against the text examples available.

3. Shared writing

The teacher models for the class how to produce some writing in the chosen genre. The pupils offer suggestions and the teacher shapes and directs their suggestions.

4. Guided writing

In the ability organised group the pupils attempt aspects of writing in the genre and present their effort to the rest of the group. The pupil has the benefit of feedback from the teacher (and peers in the group). Pupils act as 'response partners' to one another.

5. Support writing

The pupils are now ready to attempt writing in the genre but their writing will still need scaffolding to support the structure. Writing frames (for example, those produced by David Wray and Maureen Lewis) provide the necessary support at this stage. As children become more familiar with the genre the scaffolding can gradually be removed.

6. Independent writing

Children only engage in independent writing when they have moved steadily through the various stages of support. Then the pupil should have a clear idea of what is expected when writing in the particular genre and the teacher can have a high expectation of quality work.

SHARED READING AND WRITING – WORD & SENTENCE LEVEL

Many teachers have found it extremely difficult to address the needs of all abilities in Shared Word and Sentence Level work. For example, when some children are only just grasping the concept of a noun as a naming word others are ready to discuss abstract nouns. It can be very difficult to ensure that each child is being appropriately challenged.

Some teachers, who are fortunate enough to have extra help in the classroom, have arranged for one or two groups of children to practise word level work separately from the rest of the class. Other teachers have to manage the full width of the ability range and this can only successfully be undertaken if the teacher prepares word level tasks that are graded according to the children's abilities. It is very difficult to think of targeted questions off the cuff but a planned sequence of questions should mean that each child is appropriately challenged. For example when teaching children how to form adjectives from nouns, after the introduction to the whole class, challenge a more able pupil to provide an answer and then select words which conform to the same pattern, and ask a less able child to form an adjective that follows the same pattern, e.g. hopeful, helpful. Where possible word level work should take the form of an investigation. This model of teaching and learning usually provides scope for able children to contribute at their level without disadvantaging less able children.

GUIDED READING

The best approach to teaching reading is to use a balance of teaching approaches

- reading to

- reading with

- reading by

Guided reading is a 'reading with' approach. It helps readers towards a better understanding of what they are reading as the teacher guides their interaction with the text.

> *"Guided Reading involves a purposeful and pre-determined focus on reading and thinking. It is a concentrated procedure for engaging pupils with a text, supporting them in their application of reading strategies and rehearsing the behaviour of independent reading."*
>
> **First Steps Shared Reading and Writing 1 NLS Edition 1999 Heinemann**

Guided Reading involves a teacher working with a small group of children of similar ability. The teacher selects the text at an instructional level (90–95% accuracy) and provides a copy for each child. Each 20 minute session follows a similar pattern of introduction, reading the text, revisiting the text and linked word level work. Each group meets the teacher once a week for a guided session. This could focus on reading or writing.

DEVELOPING COMPREHENSION

"When reading is like spoken language and the responding is fluent, then there is a fair chance that comprehending is taking place."
Clay M. 1992

Guided reading provides the teacher with the opportunity to check that children are reading for meaning. It is very important that children expect that after they have read some pages they will stop and talk about what they have read. This is also the opportunity for the teacher to assess the child's understanding of the text.

Comprehension can be assessed in the following ways:

a) Literal comprehension, e.g.

Who are the characters in the story?

What has happened in the story?

b) Inferential comprehension, e.g.

Why do you think... happened?

What might happen next?

How do you think (the character) feels about... (event)?

c) Personal response, e.g.

What would you have done if you had been...?

Have you ever been...?

If children become familiar with the pattern of reading followed by brief discussion this can help them to remember to pay attention to the meaning of the text as they read. Occasionally instead of the teacher posing the questions to the child about the text, encourage the child to think of questions to ask the teacher.

GUIDED READING AND STRUGGLING READERS

Organising the groups

Teachers have little difficulty in organising into groups those children whose reading and writing skills are average or above average for their age, although there may be a problem accommodating an exceptionally able reader within a group. Generally teachers address this by ensuring the child's independent reading is sufficiently challenging.

However, grouping children at the lower end of the ability range can be much more difficult. These children do not fall into a homogenous group and it is not unusual for one or two struggling readers to be far below the average ability of the rest of the weak group. Not all of these very weak readers have Statements of Educational Need (although they are likely to be on the Special Needs Register at level 4). This means they may have little or no extra support in the classroom. To address this problem of grouping such diverse ability some teachers have formed groups of differing sizes, e.g. large groups (8 pupils), average groups (6 pupils) and smaller groups (2–4 pupils). Although there are some disadvantages in such small groups in terms of sharing ideas and stimulating discussion, the advantage is that the teacher can work in a concentrated way with the weakest readers, hoping to develop their skills sufficiently so that they can join another group in the future.

If these children, in the very small groups, do miss out on the benefits of peer input in Guided work, they still have the opportunity to share ideas and join in discussion in Shared Reading and Writing.

Organising books for Guided Reading

Selecting texts at an appropriate instructional level for a group of struggling readers can be very difficult. These children may not all be on the same level of text, indeed they could vary by at least two levels and yet still be well below the reading ability of the weakest child in the next group.

To address this problem of matching text level to group ability some teachers have chosen to use texts that are at instructional level for the weakest reader in the group. In order to challenge the more able readers within the group the teacher needs to ensure these pupils are asked the more discriminating questions, and when revisiting the text these children need to be encouraged to take a lead in answering the questions. (Of course all struggling readers will have the opportunity to read at their individual instructional level during the one-to-one session once a week).

Guidelines for grading books for Guided Reading

Grading books for Guided Reading for weak readers is very time-consuming and difficult. Most reading scheme books are graded according to difficulty within the terms of their own philosophy. However, many schools choose to use a wide range of different schemes to give children choice and variety. The problem arises when struggling readers are moved between beginning levels of different schemes. These readers have such a tentative grasp of reading strategies and sight vocabulary that a switch to unfamiliar characters and a change in focus of the repeated vocabulary can be very unsettling.

Although many educational publishers have produced charts showing the comparability between schemes, many struggling readers fall through the gaps.

There are some very useful publications which have graded books into a series of levels (see page 64).

Using non-fiction books

Many struggling readers feel embarrassed when they are seen reading a babyish story book and prefer to both read and be seen with non-fiction books. There are many easy to read non-fiction texts now available. These texts are written with the expectation that they will be read from beginning to end in exactly the same way as a fiction text would be read. These texts use high frequency vocabulary and repeated phrases that make them ideal texts for beginning readers. The chart on pages 48–49 suggests guidelines for matching reading ability to text difficulty.

"Many struggling readers feel embarrassed when they are seen reading a babyish story book."

A TYPICAL GUIDED READING SESSION

Each guided reading lesson should follow a similar pattern, and each part of the lesson has its own teaching and learning opportunities. The teacher needs to carefully choose an appropriate text at instructional level for the group.

1. Pre-lesson planning

The text should be one the group have not seen before. Each child will need a copy of the book.

The teacher reads the book and decides upon specific learning objectives and when these will be achieved in the Guided lesson. It may be helpful to jot these down onto a post-it note inside the back cover of the book. The teacher should select two or three children to monitor individually during the lesson. Ensure that there is a board or paper available for the teacher to write on and pupils to see.

2. During Guided Reading

Introducing the book

- Hold up a copy of the book and allow a few minutes for the children to comment on the cover, e.g. are the characters familiar? What does the title suggest? What does the cover illustration show?

- Give each child a copy of the book and, based upon the pre-determined learning objectives, draw the children's attention to unfamiliar words or concepts in the story.

- Set the children a challenge to find out something that happens in the book, e.g. find out what happens when... ...is sad. Why is he sad?

Independent reading

- Remind children of strategies they can use when they come to a word they don't know. (See What to do when you come to a word you can't read page 52).

- Tell them that if they finish before the others they are to re-read the story, with a partner if appropriate, paying particular attention to the punctuation.

- Ask the children to begin reading independently.

- While the group are reading the teacher should complete the Guided Reading Record (page 55) for the selected children.

3. After Guided Reading

- revisit the challenges set prior to the reading and check that all the children have understood the content.

- address the specific learning objective selected prior to the lesson.

These may include one or more of the following:

- check children's inferential comprehension, e.g. ask prepared questions such as "How did you know that .... was sad?"

- ask questions that require the child to relate the text to their own experiences, such as "Would you have liked to have had this happen to you?"

- select specific words from the text, e.g. that conform to a letter pattern; contain a silent letter; contain vowel digraphs; onset and rime, etc. Base teaching of these around pre-selected objectives.

- draw children's attention to features of punctuation; discuss how these affect the reading of the text.

- discuss how certain sections of the text might be read, e.g. intonation in dialogue, expression in description.

- encourage the children to pose questions of a text and ask the other children in the group to answer these.

4. Follow-up

After a Guided reading session struggling readers need the opportunity to re-read the same text. This might be supervised by a Learning Support Assistant or by the children reading with a 'buddy' and encouraged to read to each other. If the school has a policy of sending books home then it is after this second practice that the book could go home.

GUIDED WRITING AND STRUGGLING WRITERS

Guided Writing should be used as a bridge between Shared and Independent writing. The teaching strategies for Guided Writing are similar to those used for Shared Writing. The main differences are:

- the teacher does not scribe but supports the children writing for themselves

- the teaching is differentiated and individually supportive because of the smaller groups

Each Guided Writing lesson should focus upon a specific challenging aspect of writing. It is usually the case that the Shared Reading/Writing stimulus is the model for average and above average ability children; however struggling readers and writers may not be able to move from a modelled text produced in shared work to an independent piece of writing. Therefore the focus of the writing task explored in Guided Writing may not be linked to the whole class shared work. It is essential that these children are given considerable guidance before undertaking independent writing.

SUGGESTED FOCUS FOR GUIDED WRITING LESSONS

- Complete a story planner (see page 60 Story planner).

- Complete a simple Non-fiction writing frame (see pages 62–63 Writing Frames).

- Expand a simple story (see page 61).

- Punctuation (see page 59).

- Help children to write more interesting sentences. Write a simple sentence without adjectives or adverbs on the board. Show children how the sentence can be made more interesting with the addition of adjectives, adverbs, noun phrases, etc.

- Use a poetry model from a simple poem and write further verses.

- Brainstorm story openers, character descriptions, setting descriptions based on published texts.

A TYPICAL GUIDED WRITING LESSON

1. Pre-lesson planning

The teacher has to decide what writing skills the group need to practise, for example completing sentences. Prepare three or four sentence starters.

2. During Guided Writing

The teacher needs to explain carefully the learning focus of the lesson, e.g. sentences.

She writes a sentence starter on the board and then the group discuss how the sentences might be completed. As the children propose words, the teacher uses them to complete the sentence. She draws the children's attention to the spelling features of difficult words.

Independent writing during Guided Writing

Then each child completes the task set by the teacher, e.g. sentence starters.

The teacher supports with spellings where necessary but avoids dictating all the words. Instead she encourages the children to be self-reliant, reminding them of the strategies they can use when faced with spelling a difficult word. The teacher might like to use the prompt sheet 'What to do when you want to spell a word' page 57.

The teacher can also draw attention to morphemic knowledge to help children towards more accurate spelling, e.g. What do you know about the end of some past tense verbs? ('ed' not 't').

When the children have completed the sentences let them take it in turns to read them aloud. They should comment constructively on each sentence and suggest improvements for themselves and each other.

The teacher reminds the children about the focus for the session and quickly goes over what skills they have learned.

Finally the teacher needs to check that each child's draft is accurate for syntax and spellings.

3. Follow-up

After a Guided Writing session the children could either write out their writing in best handwriting, generate more spellings with an identified letter patter, or collect examples of 'ed' verbs from their reading book.

INDEPENDENT WORK

Independent work without supervision

Much of the independent work undertaken by struggling readers should be a consolidation of the skills taught in Guided Reading and Writing. These children have limited independent writing skills and if expected to complete activities that are too challenging they quickly lose interest and misbehave. Teachers are often reluctant to give them what are perceived as occupational tasks, but in order to ensure that the teacher has uninterrupted time with other groups during guided work, these 'practice' tasks are justifiable.

Possible activities might include:

* completing a relevant work sheet

* practising handwriting

* listening to taped stories and following the text

* re-reading the Guided reading book

* buddy reading

* practising known skills using the computer

Independent tasks with supervision

Many schools are endeavouring to provide adult help to work with small groups of children who are struggling with reading and writing. The phonological awareness games (page 53) and the language development games (page 54) can help oral language and vocabulary extension. In order for these games to be fully effective it is best if they are undertaken with adult supervision.

READING OUTSIDE THE LITERACY HOUR

Many schools allocate a regular block of time for children to read independently. Weak readers rarely make good use of this relatively undirected time. Although some of this time might be used by the teacher for an extended individual tuition this still leaves time when weaker readers are reading unaided. Some teachers have found that pairing children can be a very beneficial and effective use of this time.

OPTIONS FOR PAIRING

1. An able reader and a struggling reader

This can be organised within a year group or across year groups, e.g. Year 6 with Year 4, Year 5 with Year 3 etc.

The benefits of this approach are that weak readers get increased tuition and able readers get the chance to demonstrate reading skills they know implicitly. Both readers learn from the experience. Many weak readers enjoy being taught by a more skilled reader and are often more relaxed in this learning environment than they might be when taught by an adult. The text needs to be at the instructional level for the struggling reader. The able reader needs a coaching session to provide guidance on how to support their partner. This session should include:

• how to help the reader read for meaning

• how to help when the reader is stuck on a word (see page 45)

• how to discuss the text before and after reading

2. Children of similar ability

Children who have read a book in Guided Reading can re-read the same text to each other. They should be encouraged to obey the punctuation and read as fluently as possible. When they have had the opportunity to practise in this way they may like to make a recording of their reading. They should listen to the tape and evaluate their performance.

3. Group practice

Struggling readers need plenty of experience of texts below instructional level. Some teachers have found it helpful to give the group an unfamiliar text, slightly below their instructional level and to allow them 3 x 10 minutes in a week to perfect the reading. This happens without adult supervision and the children have the goal of a polished performance at the end of the week.

The group are expected to jointly sort out problem words, decide how to deliver the text and how to make the reading come alive. Because of the multiple re-readings of these texts it can be a good idea to read plays or poems. On Friday the practised text could be performed to the rest of the class.

The Role of Parents

It is not unusual to find that parents of struggling readers become less confident about how to help their children. This should not surprise us. Teachers of struggling readers are less confident about how to help them. These parents need particular support and encouragement. Many of these parents lack confidence in their own literacy skills and may feel threatened when invited to take an active role in helping their child. Sometimes these parents fail to take advantage of opportunities offered to them by the school to participate more fully in supporting their child. They do not turn up to parent evenings and may even be reluctant to talk informally to the teacher at the beginning and end of the school day. Even the home school reading diary can cause some parents anxiety. Despite their best intentions a school may fail to involve all parents. Schools can feel very frustrated by this lack of communication.

WAYS TO SUPPORT ANXIOUS PARENTS

- Do not expect these parents to hear their child read an unfamiliar, unprepared text. When parents see their child struggling with a text they do not realise why the text might be difficult, they only witness the child's failure. In their anxiety they can become cross, sometimes with the school, often with the child.

  Texts which are sent home should be ones that have either been introduced in Guided Reading or practised in supervised reading or both. The parents' role is to hear how fluently the child can read a taught text. They do not have the professional skills to teach reading strategies and should not be expected to do so.

- Rather than assessing oral reading, parent and child time should focus upon talking about the text and linking it to personal experiences. Many struggling readers are content to be word readers, if they are not challenged to respond to the text. Informal talk and chat around the book in the home, can prove the breakthrough to move these children from merely barking at print to being seekers of meaning. Parents, of course, will need to be convinced that this support is the most valuable help they can provide for their children.

- Be realistic about how many times a week and for how long parents of struggling readers can spend with their child. It is much better to ask for 2 x 5 minute sessions a week which the parents and child enjoy than to insist on a daily session which can become very stressful. Some parents might respond more enthusiastically if they were directed to help for a focused period of time, e.g. a block of six weeks. Then they need a breathing space. Providing an intensive period of support, rather than continuous commitment can take some of the pressures off parents.

- Most parents of junior aged children are not expected by the school to hear their child read to them on a regular basis although they may be asked to supervise the homework assignments. Parents of struggling readers are expected to continue the practice of sharing a book with their child, even though these older children do not happily engage in any task alongside their parents! Reading a book at home can become the focus of the child's irritation with school in general and literacy in particular. We must be sensitive to the needs of these older children.

PRACTICAL WAYS FOR PARENTS TO HELP

Send home tape versions of books for parents and children to share. If possible provide the text and the tape and ask the child to follow the text as they listen to the tape recording.

Ask the parents to encourage the children to look with them at the TV listings. Ask them to read the text with the child. This is often much more motivating than story reading!

Ask the parents to read the newspaper headlines to their children. Discuss with the child what they think about the news.

Send home homework sheets which the child can do within a reasonable amount of time. Remember homework activities should be used to consolidate knowledge and not to teach new knowledge.

"Ask the parents to read the newspaper headlines to their children."

Follow-up INSET

This section contains planning and handouts for staff INSET sessions to support the language co-ordinator when disseminating information to the staff. This could be organised into one two-hour staff meeting or four half-hour sessions.

INSET 1 Profile of a Struggling Reader (30 minutes)

What you need

Copy of page 32 'Profile of a Struggling Reader'.

Copies of Assessment Sheets pages 33–43.

1. Oral phonological knowledge: rhyme, syllables, initial letter sounds, final letter sounds, consonant clusters, medial vowels, digraphs, long vowels, blending letters.

2. Initial phoneme checklist: b c d f g h j k l m n p r s t z ch sh th wh.

3. Phonemes in medial and final position: b d f g l m n p s t - a e i o u.

4. Consonant clusters: Initial: br cr cl dr fl fr gl pl sn sp sw tr: Final: -mp -lk -nt -sk -lt -nd -st -nk.

5. Letter name knowledge; upper to lower case matching, alphabet sequence knowledge.

6. Dictated spelling of words: cvc; cvcc; ccvc; ccvcc; and vowel digraphs.

7. Read and Spell High Frequency Word List 1.

8. Read and Spell High Frequency Word Lists 2 and 3.

9. Comprehension – to reveal children who can decode words but who are failing to process the meaning of a text.

10. Attitude Questionnaire- a survey of child's perceptions about reading.

What to do

Before the INSET session

• Re-read pages 7–8, Why do Children Find Reading Difficult?

During the INSET session

• Talk to the staff about the profile of a struggling reader. Use this initial discussion and ask the staff which children fall into this category in their class.

• If appropriate include in the discussion the role of Standardised tests (page 10).

• Look at the Assessment sheets and explain the purpose of each.

Questions to consider

• What information do the staff already have about the children from other sources e.g. Key Stage 1 results, School records, Standardised tests?

• In the light of the above information what assessment do the staff feel is essential to undertake?

• Who will undertake the assessment and when will this take place?

• How will the records be used? Where will they be kept?

Struggling Readers Heinemann 2000.

Profile of a Struggling Reader

Attitude

- lacking in confidence in reading and writing

- appears to find little pleasure in reading or writing

- appears uncertain about the purpose of reading

Skills

- poorly developed cueing strategies, often relying upon a simple one letter/one sound correspondence

- lack of concern if they produce a nonsense word when decoding

- limited range of sight vocabulary

- a tendency to snatch at any word which has letters in common with a known sight word, e.g. says 'had' for 'have'

- over-reliance on illustrations to cue words, resulting in guesses which are not supported by the written word

Reading Style

- a hesitant and robotic reading aloud style which inhibits the reader from attending to the meaning

- punctuation frequently ignored

Writing Style

- can't think of anything to write

- produces minimal quantity

- muddled organisation and no desire to revise work

- little correspondence between words written and correct spelling

Response

- poor recall of content

- often reluctant to discuss what has been read

- insensitive to humour or irony in text

- little desire to read or discuss written work

Oral Assessment of Phonological Knowledge

1. **Rhyme**   Can child recognise when two words rhyme?
   door/floor   went/sent   thin/thick   dragon/flagon   brought/bring

2. **Rhyme with distracter**   Can child recognise two rhyming words out of three?
   goat/gate/coat   table/chair/stair   book/boot/cook   slide/hide/sling
   bun/ton/bin

3. **Syllables**   Can child identify number of syllables in a word?
   home   baby   window   school   video   giant   dinosaur   medal
   everybody   brought

4. **Initial letter sounds**   Can child identify initial letter sounds?
   sun   ant   up   cab   hug   egg   lid   nut   rat   bat   zip   tap   ink
   odd   van   fan   wall   jam

5. **Final letter sounds**   Can child identify final letter sounds?
   pan   fill   tub   pet   cliff   bus   bad   wig   ham   top

6. **Consonant clusters**   Can child identify both letters in the consonant clusters?
   black   plum   trap   brown   slide   grape   spill   clap   print   glass
   flag   swim   crab   stop

7. **Medial vowels**   Can child identify medial vowel sound?
   bag   beg   big   bog   bug

8. **Initial and Final digraphs**   Can child identify digraphs?
   ship   thin   chin   when   initial

   fish   coach   with   black   end

9. **Blending phonemes**   Can child blend given sounds of letters together?
   c – a – b   p – e – t   l – i – d   h – o – t   b – u – t

   s – p – e – ll   g – r – a – b   w – e – n – t   j – u – m – p
   p – l – o – t

   d – r – i – n – k   s – p – e – l – t   s – l – u – m – p   s – w – i – f – t
   b – l – u – n – t

10. **Long vowel sound**   Can child identify long vowel sound?
    face   home   tries   hail   seed   blue   cheat   mice   cube   road

Struggling Readers   Heinemann 2000.   Copyright permitted for purchasing school only. This material is not copyright free.

33

NAME:

NAME:

DATE:

Initial Phoneme Check List

Circle the initial letter sound.

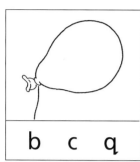

b   c   q

g   s   c

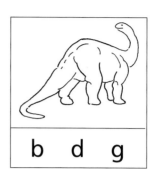

b   d   g

h   f   t

g   p   h

n   h   b

h   i   j

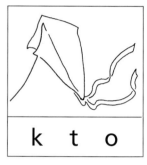

k   t   o

h   l   i

m   n   w

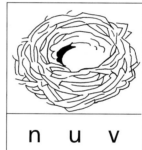

n   u   v

p   q   b

s   z   a

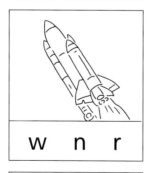

w   n   r

t   s   n

f   r   t

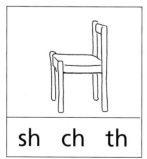

sh   ch   th

wh   ch   sh

th   wh   sh

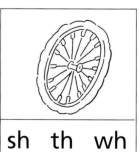

sh   th   wh

Final Phoneme Check List

Circle the final letter sound.

		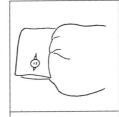		
b c d	h d e	u c f	g a u	l w h
		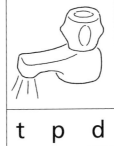	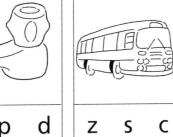	
n p m	n c p	t p d	z s c	f t b

Vowel Check List

Circle the initial letter sound.

			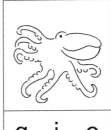	
e a i	e o u	a i e	a i o	a i u

Circle the middle letter sound.

	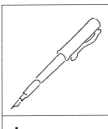			
a u i	i e o	u o i	a u o	u e a

Struggling Readers   Heinemann 2000.

NAME:	DATE:
....	....

Consonant Cluster Check List

Write the beginning consonant cluster under the picture.

br- cr- cl- dr- fl- fr- gl- pl- sn- sp- sw- tr-

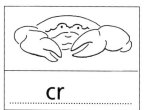

cr

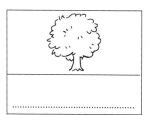 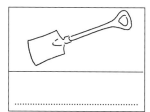 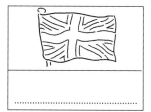

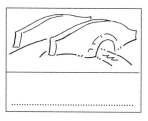 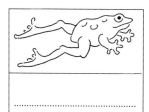 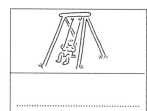 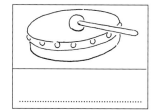

 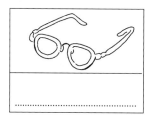 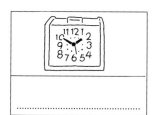 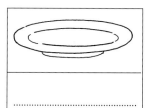

Write the final consonant cluster under the picture.

-mp -lt -nd -sk -nt -lk -st -nk

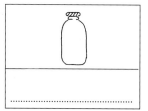 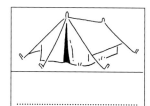 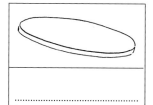 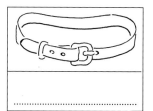

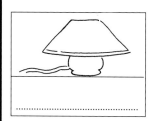   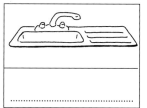

Upper case/Lower case letter names

Name each of the upper and lower case letters.

Then draw a line to link the upper case letter to its lower case partner.

| A | F | J | B | G | K | C | H | L | D | I | E | M |

| j | b | f | a | k | c | g | h | l | m | e | i |

| N | S | X | O | T | Y | P | U | Q | V | R | W | Z |

| x | n | o | s | y | t | u | p | v | q | z | r | w |

Alphabet Order

Fill in the gaps.

| a b c __ e | l m n __ p | g __ i j k | e __ g __ i |

| s t u v __ x | g h i __ k | j k l __ n | q r s __ u |

Write the alphabet in order.

....

37

NAME:	DATE:

Dictation: Spelling Regular Words

Dictate the following words.

CVC Words: *vowel in initial position*

ant   end   ink   ox   up

CVC Words: *vowel in medial position*

sad   leg   bin   top   run

CVCC Words

land   belt   sank   held   hurt   jump   vest

dent   milk   lisp   disk   help

CCVC Words

grab   clap   stop   pram   drum   swim   flan   crab

snap   glum   trip   spit   from   blot   twin   brim

Long Vowel Sounds

wait   late   day

feet   heat

pie   bite   high

boat   bone   blow

few   cube

High Frequency Words List 1

	Read	Spell		Read	Spell		Read	Spell		Read	Spell
I			in			dog			like		
a			of			big			said		
we			it			mum			this		
on			me			dad			they		
at			all			all			away		
he			and			get			play		
is			for			was			come		
go			you			she			went		
am			are			see			going		
to			cat			yes					
my			day			can					
no			the			look					

High Frequency Words List 2

	Read	Spell		Read	Spell		Read	Spell		Read	Spell
an			good			more			ran		
as			got			must			saw		
back			had			name			seen		
ball			has			new			so		
be			have			next			take		
bed			help			night			than		
been			her			not			that		
boy			here			now			then		
but			him			off			three		
by			his			old			too		
came			home			once			took		
can't			how			one			tree		
did			if			or			two		
do			jump			our			us		
don't			just			out			very		
dig			last			over			want		
door			make			push			way		
from			man			pull			were		
girl			may			put			what		

High Frequency Words List 3

	Read	Spell		Read	Spell		Read	Spell		Read	Spell
about			much			one			Sunday		
after			people			twelve			Friday		
again			school			six			Saturday		
another			should			three			Monday		
because			sister			five			Wednesday		
brother			some			nine			Thursday		
called			their			seven			Tuesday		
could			them			eleven			December		
down			there			two			June		
first			time			four			July		
half			water			eight			September		
house			when			ten			January		
laugh			where			blue			March		
little			who			red			May		
lived			will			green			October		
love			with			yellow			November		
made			would			black			February		
many			your			white			April		
						orange			August		

NAME:	DATE:

Comprehension

Tick the correct sentence.

The cat is in the box. ☐

The cat is on the box. ☐

The bird has got a worm. ☐

The bird has not got a worm. ☐

The dog is on the hat. ☐

The hat is on the dog. ☐

The boy has two footballs. ☐

The two boys have a football. ☐

Do these sentences mean the same thing?

The cow is in the field with the horse.

The cow and the horse are in the field.   Yes   No

The man and the boy got on the bus.

The man got off the bus and the boy got on.   Yes   No

The car is going fast round the corner.

The fast car is going round the corner.   Yes   No

"Mum," said Jo "Where is my hat?"

Mum said "Jo, where is my hat?"   Yes   No

NAME:	DATE:

Attitude Questionnaire

Do you have a favourite book? ....

Are you a good reader? ....

What do good readers do? ....

What do you like best about reading? ....

....

What do you not like about reading? ....

....

Do you like reading to your teacher? ....

Do you read at home? ....

Who with? ....

What happens? ....

What do you do when you come to a word you don't recognise?

....

Do you think reading is important? ....

Why? ....

How could you become a better reader? ....

....

INSET 2   Hearing Children Read

What you need

1. Copies of 'Pause, Prompt and Praise' page 45.

2. Copies of 'The 10 Minute Individual Teaching Session' page 46.

3. Copies of 'How to Teach Spelling from Identified Miscues' page 47.

4. Copies of Guidelines for matching reading ability to text difficulty pages 48–49.

5. A range of the fiction and non-fiction books used with Struggling Readers.

What to do

Before the INSET session

Re-read pages 10–13 Assessing Oral Reading.

During the INSET session

- Ask the staff what they currently do with the children who are causing concern.

- Go through 'Pause, Prompt and Praise' page 45.

- Explain to the staff how to undertake the 10 minute individual session.

- Go through the level descriptors and discuss how to match the child with the book.

- Ask the staff to allocate a sample of the books to the level descriptors.

Questions to consider

- How often is it necessary to hear these children read?

- Who should listen to the children read?

- What other adults are available to support these children's reading?
  What approach do the staff want these adults to use? e.g. Pause, Prompt and Praise?

- How many children should undertake the extended 10 minute sessions?

- When will time be available?

- Are the texts that the children read interesting and exciting?

- Do the available books match all the different levels?

- Have other children in the class read these books in the Infant school?

- Is there a good choice of fiction and non-fiction?

- Where are the gaps in the resources and what should be prioritised when funds are available?

Pause, Prompt and Praise

Tutoring Procedure

What to do when a child makes an error

For Correct Reading

1. We should praise when children read a sentence correctly

2. We should praise when children correct themselves after a mistake

3. We should praise when children get a word correct after we have prompted them

For Problem Reading

1. We should wait to give children a chance to solve the problem

If the Mistake Does Not Make Sense

2. We should prompt with clues about the meaning of the story

e.g. we should ask a question

If the Mistake Does Make Sense

3. We should prompt with clues about the way the words look

e.g. we should ask about one part that is wrong

If the Child Says Nothing

4. We should ask the child to read on to the end of the sentence

or, we should ask the child to go back to the beginning of the sentence again

If the Word is not Correct After Two Prompts

5. We should say "The word is ..."

Derived from S. Colmar & K. Wheldall, Three Ps for the effective tutoring of low progress readers: Pause, Prompt and Praise, in *Prevention of Reading Failure*, edited by A.J. Watson and A.M. Badenhop (Aston Scholastic, 1992)

The 10 Minute Individual Teaching Session

You will need:

- one or two titles at child's instructional level

- paper and pencil for child

- paper and pen to record miscues

2 minutes: Prepared Reading

- Ask child to quickly select book to read.

- Go through the book using the Prepared Reading approach.

4 minutes: Hearing the child read

- Ask the child to read aloud. Explain that you want them to try to read all the words.

- Listen to the child's reading and note any problems (e.g. miscues, pace, fluency, punctuation)

4 minutes: Teaching linked to identified miscues

- Show the child a page where a problem occurred and discuss the word.

EITHER FOCUS A: common letter patterns

- Select a problem word which has a regular onset and rime pattern and show child how to generate other words
e.g. went/bent/sent.

OR FOCUS B: high frequency words

- Select an irregular high frequency word that has given child a problem. Encourage child to write word from memory by 'look, say, see, cover, write, check' approach.

How to Teach Spelling From Identified Miscues

You will need:

- The book the child has read to you
- Paper
- Pencil

What to do – Focus A: common letter patterns

1. From the book the child has just read select a sentence which includes a word with a common rime, e.g. He sat on the w<u>all</u>.

2. Ask the child to read the sentence.

3. Tell the child to study the word 'wall' and then to write it from memory.

4. Show the child the connection between 'wall' and call, fall, ball, stall.

This procedure helps children to see the pattens in words and it 'unlocks' new words.

What to do – Focus B: high frequency words

1. From the book the child has just read choose a sentence which contains a high frequency 'irregular' word e.g. "<u>They</u> could not get the cat".

2. Ask the child to read the sentence.

3. Ask the child to attempt any words they know from memory e.g. not, get, the cat.

4. Write any 'difficult' word for the child that you are not focusing upon e.g. could.

5. Teach the child to spell the selected word "they" – look at the word, finger trace the word onto a tactile surface, say the letter names, write the word from memory onto paper.

6. Ask the child to write the complete sentence from memory (except any difficult word not selected).

This procedure helps children to learn high frequency words which are not phonetically regular.

Struggling Readers Heinemann 2000. Copyright permitted for purchasing school only. This material is not copyright free.

Guidelines for matching reading ability with text difficulty

Working within Level 1
Reader's profile

- recognises approximately 20 high frequency words
- uses initial letter sounds to guess at unfamiliar words
- accurately points at each word
- has minimal grasp of story content
- no evidence of self-correcting
- ignores punctuation
- reads aloud in a robotic way

Text features

- 1–2 lines of text using high frequency vocabulary and repetition between pages
- 1–3 lines of text using high frequency vocabulary within the page
- highly predictable story line
- nouns are picture-cued
- most of the text is dialogue and echoes children's spoken language

Working towards Level 2
Reader's profile

- recognises approximately 50 high frequency words
- beginning to use sounding out and blending strategies
- can recall basic features of simple plot
- self-corrects when prompted
- recognises the function of full stops and capital letters
- reads aloud in a monotone

Text features

- 1–3 lines of text using high frequency vocabulary and some repetition between pages
- 2–4 lines of text using high frequency vocabulary and some repetition between pages
- predictable story line
- nouns are picture-cued
- most of the text is in dialogue and echoes children's spoken language

Working within Level 2
Reader's profile

- recognises approximately 120 words
- uses sounding out and blending more accurately
- recalls main events and can comment on them
- begins to self-correct without prompting
- recognises the function of speech marks
- reads aloud slowly but with some intonation and expression

Text features

- up to 6 lines of text, with some high frequency vocabulary and some repetition
- story lines still predictable but with more events
- key nouns are picture-cued
- text is a mixture of narrative and dialogue and may include adjectives
- sentences are of varied length
- introduction of technical vocabulary in non-fiction texts

Guidelines for matching reading ability with text difficulty

Working towards Level 3

Reader's profile

- recognises approximately 200 sight words
- processes all sounds to read unknown words
- can follow all aspects of a plot and respond imaginatively
- self-corrects automatically
- reads aloud with some fluency but tends to vocalise when reading alone

Text features

- 6–12 lines and some whole pages of text
- text more dense and fewer illustrations
- more subtle link between illustrations and text
- plots have more than one strand
- texts include sustained narrative and some descriptive passages
- sentences include subordinate clauses
- greater use of technical vocabulary in non-fiction

Working within Level 3

Reader's profile

- recognises approximately 200 sight words
- processes all sounds to read an unknown word
- can follow all aspects of a plot and respond imaginatively
- responds to most punctuation including commas and exclamation marks
- reads silently
- is aware of requirements when reading aloud to others

Text features

- fiction is divided into chapters and requires reading stamina
- illustrations occasional and decorative
- plots are more complex
- characterisation is more subtle and requires interpretation
- text includes literary and poetic language
- texts employ a wide range of connectives, e.g. however, since, although
- non-fiction vocabulary may be challenging. Reader must interpret diagrams and charts

Working towards Level 4

Reader's profile

- responds to irony and figurative language
- predicts imaginatively, makes inferences, reads between the lines
- beginning to distinguish between author and narrator
- confidently uses all cueing strategies
- growing awareness of how different texts work
- able to use contents, index and glossary to access information

Text features

- fiction is lengthy and sustained and it requires reader commitment
- illustrations are minimal
- several strands of a plot run simultaneously
- characterisation is more subtle and requires interpretation
- texts may include dialects
- reads and understands genre of non-fiction texts

Struggling Readers Heinemann 2000.

INSET 3   Shared and Guided Reading

What you need

1. Copies of 'Levels of Comprehension' page 51.

2. Copies of the flow chart 'What to do when you come to a word you can't read' page 52.

3. A Big Book.

4. Copies of the 'Phonological Games' page 53.

5. Copies of the 'Language Development Games' page 54.

6. A selection of texts suitable for Guided Reading with Struggling Readers.

7. Guided Reading Record page 55.

What to do

Before the INSET session

Re-read pages 14–22 Shared and Guided Reading.

Prepare questions from the Big Book to demonstrate the levels of comprehension.

During the INSET session

- Go through the handout 'Levels of Comprehension'.

- Demonstrate from the Big Book the different types of questions.

- Discuss with the staff ways of involving weak readers in the whole class Shared Reading sessions.

- Remind the staff about the structure of a Guided Reading session.

- Remind staff of ways to judge the difficulty of a text and ask them to select a text and work with a partner to decide upon the specific learning objective for the text.

- Remind staff of ways of prompting the children to use the different reading strategies and look at the chart.

- Draw the staff's attention to the "Phonological Games" and "Language Development Games".

- Discuss the 'Guided Reading Record' and how it can be used in the classroom.

Questions to ask

Are the children participating in the whole class Shared Reading?

If not, how can the teacher ensure that they are taking an active part in the lesson?

Are the children responding to the content of the book as well as decoding the texts in Guided Reading? If not how can they be encouraged to respond?

Levels of Comprehension

"The reader constructs meaning by making connectives between what the author has written and what the reader knows." **Makill J. 1999**

Comprehension occurs when readers are required to reflect upon what they have read. We must encourage children to ask themselves as they read:

"What does this mean?"

"What is going to happen next?"

"What should the character have done?"

"What would I have done?"

The levels of comprehension are often referred to as:

- **reading the lines**

- **reading between the lines**

- **reading beyond the lines**

Reading the lines (Literal Comprehension)

This involves retaining the information provided explicitly by the text. The child needs to establish what information the author gave, e.g. names of characters, setting, and events.

Reading between the lines (Interpretative Comprehension)

This requires the child to interpret implications in the text and make judgements based on the information given, e.g. whether a character is good or bad, whether an action was sensible or foolish.

Reading beyond the lines (Applied Comprehension)

This requires the child to link events to his or her own experiences and possibly to speculate about those experiences, e.g. what would they have done in a similar situation, what do they think might happen next.

Struggling Readers Heinemann 2000.

What to do when you can't read a word

1. Look at the first few letters and the last letter – can you think of the word?
   Does it make sense?

| | Well done! You've worked out the word. |

2. Sound out the letters – can you blend them into a word you know?

| | Does it make sense? Yes? Great! No? Try this |

3. Divide the word into syllables.
   Can you see letter combinations that you recognise?

| | Can you blend them together? Is it a word that fits? |

4. Look at the picture. Does it give you a clue?

| | Does it make sense? Yes? Great! No? Try this |

5. Read the sentence again and miss out the word.
   Can you think what word might go in the gap?

6. Read the whole sentence including the word you have put in – does it make sense?

   Yes = carry on reading
   No = ask an adult for help

Phonological Games

1. **Guess the rhyming word**
   Make up short rhyming couplets, ask the children to complete with rhyming words.
   Mr. Down   Open the door   Can you see the cat   I have been told
   Went to ____   And sit on the ____   Wearing a ____   Of some pirates ____

2. **Spot the rhyming pairs**
   Present children with group of three words of which two rhyme. Ask them to tell
   you the rhyming pair.   Seat/tree/bee   rug/chair/bug   black/sack/king

   Increase the difficulty by making the distracter start with the same letter
   cup/can/pan   flag/drag/flip   mouse/mice/house

3. **Complete the clue**
   Tell the children that you are thinking of a word which rhymes with...
   I am thinking of a word that rhymes with red.   You go to sleep in this
   I am thinking of a word that rhymes with fool.   You go there every weekday

4. **Silly stories**
   Retell a well known traditional tale but change some words with rhyming
   alternatives. For example "Once upon a crime there was a ring who had a beautiful
   daughter. The sing gave her everything she wanted. One play she asked him for a
   golden call..."
   The children should tell you when you have made a mistake and tell you the
   rhyming 'correct' word. Some older children could be given this story to read and
   'correct'.

5. **Alliteration lines**
   Help the children to make up alliterative sentences.
   Mike makes many mice move merrily   Sophie saw seven swans swimming silently

6. **Rhyming Pairs**
   Make wall displays of rhyming pairs. Show the children when the rhyming words
   also have a common pattern and when the words sound alike but have a different
   letter pattern. e.g. make/take   seat/meet
   Display on the classroom wall, preferably near the door where children line up as
   this encourages both reading and discussion.

7. **Syllable game**
   Tell the group you are going to say some words and they are to tell you how many
   syllables they can hear. Show them that breaking a word into syllables can help with
   spelling, e.g. today   sitting   helpful   quickly   opened   morning   began
   different   something   number   suddenly   together   Sunday   sixteen.

Language Development Games

1. **Create a known story**
   Take a well-known story and ask the children to help you to retell the story. Start the story off and then ask the children in the group to continue. For example, One day little Red Riding Hood's mother called to her and said ... Child 1. "Take this basket of food to your grandmother..."

2. **Create a new story.**
   Start a new story with the group and ask them to continue to develop it. For example, "Once upon a time there was a little old man who lived in a tumbled down cottage. One day he said to himself..." If possible tape record the story.

3. **Sequence your story**
   Explain to the group that the publisher has asked for illustrations to go with their stories. Ask them to sequence the story and decide which parts should be illustrated. (If the illustrations are equal to the number of children in the group you could suggest that each child selects a page for illustration and that they write a caption text under their picture. This could be done in independent time.)

4. **True or false?**
   Tell the group that you are going to say some sentences that are true or not true. They should listen to the sentence and then decide whether it is true or not, e.g. There are 5 children in this group. A dog can fly. I wear glasses. There will be no lunch today. I can't see any books in this classroom.

5. **Synonyms**
   Write some appropriate words onto cards and place them face down on the table. Ask each child to take it in turns to pick up a card and think of a synonym. For each accurate word they suggest give them a counter. The winner is the child with the most counters. Suggested words: nice; sad; said; cross; happy; big; small; good; bad. Finally show the children how to find other words using a thesaurus.

6. **Asking questions**
   Write each of the following words onto a card: who; what; where; why; when. Place the cards face down and ask the children to take it in turns to pick up a card. They should then ask a question starting with their selected word. Write their questions onto a board and discuss how to punctuate the sentence.

7. **Alphabet Adverbs**
   Write a sentence on the board containing an active verb and ask the group to suggest adverbs to modify the verb. The group could either suggest an adverb starting with the same letter of the alphabet or progress through the alphabet.
   e.g. The boy spoke angrily/anxiously/attractively.
   The girl ran agilely/badly/carefully/disastrously/effectively.

Guided Reading Record

Group: _____ Date: _____

Book title: _____ Genre: _____

Key teaching objectives:

- _____
- _____
- _____

	Reading Assessment				
	During reading **Reading performance**		**Before/After reading** **Response & Understanding**		
Name	cueing strategies	reading with expression	literal comprehension	inferential comprehension	personal response

Comments:

Follow-up activities: (circle as appropriate)

Related Guided Writing   pcm   re-read in Independent Work

Read next chapter   Other _____

What next?

- Re-visit teaching objectives
- Ensure _____ receive further support
- Alter group composition
- OA follow-up

INSET 4 Developing Writing Skills (30 minutes)

What you need

1. Copies of the flow chart 'What to do when you want to spell a word' page 57.

2. Copies of 'Ways to learn tricky words' page 58.

3. Copies of the punctuation chart page 59.

4. Copies of the 'Story planner' and 'Simple Story outlines' pages 60 and 61.

5. Copies of the writing frames pages 62 and 63.

What to do

Before the INSET session

Re-read pages 23–24 Guided Writing and pages 15–17 Shared Writing.

During the INSET session

- Talk to the staff about the stages of teaching and learning when introducing a genre (pages 15–16).

- Remind staff about the typical ingredients of a Guided Writing session.

- Discuss with the staff the focus that a lesson might take.

- Look at the writing frames for Non-fiction writing.

- Look at the suggestions for sentence development.

- Look at the 'Story planner' and the 'Simple story outlines'.

Questions to consider

What can struggling writers do after a Guided Writing session?

How often should struggling writers be asked to undertake an extended writing session?

How will the focused spelling tasks fit into the school's spelling policy?

Are there issues about poor handwriting and weak writers?

What to do when you want to spell a word

1. How many sounds you can hear in the word.

2. Write a letter for each sound.

> Don't forget some sounds need two or more letters.

3. Decide how many syllables you can hear in the word.

4. Write down the first and last letters in the word or the syllable.

> You could write the letters and leave a line in between

5. Do you know any other word that has the same letter sounds in it?

> Write down the word trying different ways of writing the letter sounds

6. Write down the word trying different ways of writing the letter sounds.

7. Decide which of the spellings you have tried looks the best.

8. If possible check this spelling in a dictionary.

9. Read what you have written. Does it look right?

10. Still need help? Ask an adult.

Ways to learn tricky words

- Look at the word.

- Read the word.

- Say the names of the letters to yourself three times.

- Close your eyes and 'see' the word.

- Write the word onto a tactile surface with your index finger.

- Write the word onto paper without copying.

- Check the spelling.

- Try to write the word again from memory later in the day.

Ask a friend to test you on your new word.

Don't forget your punctuation!

Remember

- Every sentence starts with a capital letter and ends with a full stop.

capital letter → The children went out to play. ← full stop

- People's names, places, days of the week and months of the year start with a capital letter.

→ Mr. Jones went to London on Monday, January 10th.

capital letters

- If you ask a question you must put a question mark at the end of the sentence.

Where must you put a question mark?

- When somebody speaks you must put speech marks around the words they say.

"Don't forget the speech marks," said the teacher.

- Put commas between items on a list but NOT before 'and'.

Now you know about capital letters, full stops, question marks and speech marks.

Struggling Readers Heinemann 2000. Copyright permitted for purchasing school only. This material is not copyright free.

Story planner

Characters names:

....

....

....

....

What my characters are like

happy   sad   careful   unlucky   clever

brave   strong   kind   mean   honest

funny   messy   horrible   timid   sensible

Other ....

Where my story takes place:

....

....

Settings

town   country   night   day   school

seaside   mountain   alien   planet   home

in the future   in the past   today

Other ....

What happens:

....

....

....

Problems

a quarrel?   someone is lost?

something is stolen?   an accident?

parents do not want your pet?   have 3 wishes

Other ....

How my story ends:

....

....

....

....

Solution

find the treasure   make friends

someone helps you home   find a new pet

you end up in hospital   live happily ever after

Simple Story Outlines

Many struggling writers find planning a story and keeping to that plan very difficult. The following simple story outlines may help them to become more familiar with the structure of the narrative form. It is suggested that the teacher provides the outline sentences and writes these onto A4 paper leaving a good space in between each section for the child to write in.

The children need to realise that the story outlines need complications and satisfactory resolutions so that the readers wants to find out what happens.

What to do

1. Give each child a copy of the story outline.

2. Explain to the group that they are going to draft their own story based around the story outline.

3. Ask the group to think about who is in the story, where the story takes place, when it takes place, how the character feels and what happens.

4. Discuss with the group ways of expanding the introduction to include details of the characters and the setting.

5. Tell the group to write their own opening paragraph.

6. Ask each member of the group to read out their opening. Encourage other members of the group to comment constructively and help the writer to improve their sentences.

7. Discuss possible developments for the remaining sections.

8. Help with spelling and grammar. Ensure that each child has a correctly spelled and grammatically accurate first paragraph at the end of the session.

9. Tell the group to copy out their story opening in independent time in their best handwriting.

10. In subsequent Guided Writing Lessons go through the same procedure, concentrating on linking story complications to satisfactory resolutions or own story endings.

Possible story outlines

Two friends build a rocket	A boy goes for a walk
They fly to another planet	He gets lost
They land on the planet	He meets a friend
They return to earth	They find the way home
A monster hatches from an egg	Two friends go on holiday
It starts to eat everything in sight	They find a cave in the side of the cliff
It finishes all the food	They find some treasure
It meets another monster	They take the treasure to a museum

NAME:	DATE:
....	....

Explanation Writing Frame

Useful words for this subject

Introduction

I am going to explain ....
....
....

Remember to say 'how' or 'what happens'

Paragraph 1

....
....
....

Remember to give your evidence. You might say when or then…

Paragraph 2

Another reason is ....
....
....

Remember you might like to use 'next' or 'after this'

Paragraph 3

The result is

....

Discussion Writing Frame

Useful words for this discussion

Introduction

In our class we have been discussing ....

....

....

> You might like to use words like 'because' 'when' 'agree' 'argue'

Paragraph 1

Some children think ....

....

....

Paragraph 2

Other children think ....

....

....

Paragraph 3

I think that ....

> You could use 'in my opinion'

....

Futher Reading

Bentley D. Reid D. 1995 Supporting Struggling Readers   UKRA
Bindon R. 1999 First Steps: Shared and Guided Reading and Writing 2   Heinemann
Clay M 1991 Becoming Literate: The contruction of inner control   Heinemann
Dewsbury A. 1999 First Steps: Shared and Guided Reading and Writing 1   Heinemann
Eldon E. Shanker J. 1993 Locating and Correcting Reading Difficulties   Merrill USA
Goodwin P. (ed) 1999 The Literate Classroom   Fulton
Layton L. Deeny K. Upton G. 1997 Sound Practice: Phonological Awareness in the classroom
Makgill J. 1999 Guided reading: Going Solo under instruction   UKRA
Reason R. Boote R. 1994 Helping Children with Reading and Spelling   Routledge

Graded Lists of Reading Books

Book Bands for Guided Reading: organising Key Stage One texts for the Literacy Hour 1998 Reading Recovery National Network, 20 Bedford Way, London WC1H OAL.
This has graded fiction and non-fiction books from both reading series and trade books into 10 bands. This grading covers books suitable for children 'Working towards Level1' of the National Curriculum Levels to 'Working towards Level 3'. This is a very useful publication but teachers should be aware that these books were selected for a younger group of children and some content may appear too childish for older weak readers.

The Catch Up Non-fiction Book List. 1999 The Catch Up Project, School of Education, Oxford Brookes University, Wheatley Campus, Oxford OX33 1HX.
This has graded easy to read non-fiction books into 9 levels of difficulty. This booklet was designed especially for weak readers in Years 3/4 and covers books suitable for children 'Working towards Level 1' of the National Curriculum levels to 'Working towards Level 3'.

Individualised Reading (Published Annually) The Reading and Language Information Centre, University of Reading, Bulmershe Court, Earley, Reading RG5 1HY.
This grades recommended fiction and poetry from both reading schemes and trade books into 13 levels. It has targeted average readers from 5–11 years. It contains many titles that could be used with reluctant readers but these are not indicated. The teacher will need to check the suitability of the titles.

The NASEN A–Z: A Graded list of Reading Books 1997 NASEN Enterprises Ltd, NASEN House, 4/5 Amber Business Village, Amber Close, Amington, Tamworth, Staffs B77 4RP.
This lists educational books for children between 5 and 11 years and allocates them a reading age, interest age and phase. This means that teachers can quickly select books suitable for older reluctant readers. The books have been graded using professional knowledge, the use of cloze procedure and the use of a readability formula. This publication is also available on CD-ROM.